FREEDOM PASSAGE

A Memoir by Christina Victoria

Copyright Page – *Freedom Passage*

Cover design by Christina Victoria
Published by: Marion Alexander Press
Printed in the United States of America

ISBN: 9798993982502
LCCN: 2025925816

MAP Edition: 2025
Freedom Passage | www.marionalexanderpress.com

Dedication

For my sons, who taught me grace.

For my younger self, who carried so much.

For my father, whose absence shaped my strength.

And for the woman still learning how to choose herself—this passage is for you.

Acknowledgments

To *God*—thank you for my pen, my purpose, and my protection. You have held me together through every unraveling.

To my sons—*Christopher and Cortes*. You are the joy I never knew I needed, the light that kept me going when everything else felt dark. You gave my life purpose and color. I hope one day you'll read these pages and understand just how much you saved me, just by being mine.

To my village—you know who you are. Those who stood in the gaps, sent the texts, made the calls, and reminded me I didn't have to be strong all the time. Thank you for loving me in real time.

To *Whitney*—thank you for showing up in my life the way you did. Thank you for the way you see me, speak life into me, and stand beside me in both the glow and the grit.

To the little girl I used to be, I see you. I hear you. And I wrote this book for you.

And to you, the reader, thank you for holding my story. I hope these pages remind you that your voice matters, your healing is sacred, and your freedom is yours to define.

Author's Reflection: How It Started

I didn't plan to write this book, I needed to.

For years, my stories lived inside of me like whispers.

I knew they were there, but I was too busy surviving to stop and listen.

Too busy caregiving, showing up for everyone else, and holding in the truth of what I had endured.

One day, I started writing letters.

Not formal ones—just raw, messy entries in my notes app.
Sentences that didn't make sense at first.
Feelings I couldn't say out loud, but my fingers knew how to type.

I wrote in waiting rooms.
In my car.
On the edge of my bed while the world slept and I couldn't.

Slowly, those pieces became something.
And I began to remember the woman I was before life told me to be quiet.

Writing didn't just give me a voice.

It gave me back myself.

I wrote my way through grief, through survival, through silence.
And page by page, I found something deeper than healing—I found clarity, courage, and freedom that could only come from telling the truth.

This reflection is not about how polished the journey looks.

It's about how powerful it is to even begin.

If you're reading this, I want you to know:
Your story matters.

Your softness matters.

Your freedom matters.

And if you've ever lost your voice… this is your permission to find it again.

Sending Light & Love

~ Christina

Introduction:

Freedom Passage

This book is more than a memoir—it is a passage.

A collection of letters written in the dark, lit by healing, shaped by becoming, and stitched together with the bold return to myself.

Each letter you'll read is a small rebellion.

A moment where I chose healing over hiding, becoming over breaking, and truth over silence.
That's what this passage is.
That's what this freedom is.

I didn't write this for perfection.

I wrote this for the woman who has stayed too long in places that dim her light.

I wrote this for the mothers who have poured from an empty cup with grace they were never given.

I wrote this for the dreamers, the quiet survivors, the women who cry in bathrooms, who show up anyway, and who are still learning how to choose themselves without apology.

I didn't always have the language for what I was carrying.

So, I started writing letters to myself, to my sons, to the versions of me I had buried along the way.

This book holds those letters—raw, reflective, unfinished at times, but always true.

You won't find a perfect arc here.

You'll find fragments. Memories. Moments that broke me
open.

Stories that started as scribbles on my phone between hospital
visits and heartbreaks.

Chapters I didn't want to write—but needed to, if I was ever
going to feel whole.

Some of these pages will feel like prayers.
Some like declarations.
Some like standing in the mirror for the first time after
surviving something you never told anyone about.
This book is not linear.
It is layered, like all of us.

But if you follow the thread, you'll see the journey: from silence
to voice, from survival to glow, from aching to agency.

Freedom Passage is not just mine.

It is for every woman who has wondered if she was asking for
too much—when really, she was asking for what should have
always been sacred: peace, presence, protection, and love that
doesn't require shrinking.

I don't know where you are on your journey.
But if you're here, I hope something in these pages reminds you
of who you are.

I hope it gives you permission to rest, to release, to remember.

Because your glow was never gone.

It was just waiting for the passage back to you.

With love and truth,
~ Christina

Inside the Passage

Freedom Passage — A Memoir by Christina Victoria

Part I: The Becoming
Healing, Self-Discovery, and Childhood Roots

1.I Carried Bruises No One Could See

2. What Was Buried, Bloomed Anyway

3. Raised by My Sons

4. Christopher, My First Home

5. Cortes, the Love That Completed Me

6. My Spirit Kissed the Earth

7. Sunlight and Shoulder Blades

8. I Showed Up

9. Ode to PTC (Peachtree City)

Part II: The Breaking
Love, Loss, and Letting Go

10. He Didn't Deserve Me

11. Do You Love Him?

12. It Wasn't All Bad

13. In the Space Between (*echo poem*)

14. Fairytales

15. I Cried for Miles

16. The Truth Is Buried with Him

17. All I Have Are Pieces

18. *Glow Scene:* * The Woman Who Stayed

19. The Love Bar

Part III: The Reclaiming
Voice, Power, and Return to Self

20. Glow Up Chronicles

21. Fupa and Freedom

22. Sunday Morning Rituals

23. Survival Works (But Damn, It Hurts)

24. *Glow Scene:* The Power in My Eyes

25. Peace, Partnership, and Presence

Part IV: The Rising
Confidence, Clarity, and Grown-Woman Glow

26. The Glow in the Galaxy

27. Reclaiming Me

28. Comfort for Conversation

29. No Fall-Back Plan

30. My Sons Were My Applause

31. Legacy Notes (standalone reflection)

Part V: The Passage
Softness, Closure, and Becoming Whole

32. No Villains

33. *Glow Scene*: Beautiful Things, Empty Rooms

34. The Story That is Sold (*Reflection on Performance, Perception, and Emotional Capitalism*)

35. The Final Passage

Part I: THE BECOMING

Healing, Self-Discovery, and Childhood Roots

Chapter 1

I Carried Bruises No One Could See

Author's Note:

This chapter holds truths I once buried. I write this not to accuse, but to release. This is not a story of blame—it's a story of survival.

We carry too many secrets in Black families.
And we let too many things live in silence.

We say things like:
"Don't leave the kids at Uncle Johnny's house."
Or "Aunt Velma's just a little touched."
We whisper warnings—coded and cautious—
but we rarely call it what it is.

Because naming it out loud
means confronting all the ways we weren't protected.
It means facing the trauma we inherited
before we ever knew how to keep anyone else safe.

Church told us to pray about it.
Generations taught us therapy was for the broken.
So we carried our pain like bones in a velvet bag—
hidden, heavy, and passed down.

I was four.
She was the neighbor.
To this day, she feels like something from a nightmare circus.
I cried hysterically when you left me with her.

Instead of listening,
you punished me.

Told me to stop all that damn crying.

Did you know?
Did Daddy know?
Wasn't my screaming a sign?

Four years later, he died.
The greatest loss of my childhood.
And somewhere in that grief,
I felt the shift—like maybe you resented me for surviving him.
I would grow to resent you for it too.

When I was twelve,
I told you the truth.
Not about Daddy.
Another man.
Someone who should've never had access to me.

His touch wasn't accidental.
It was deliberate.
Violating.
Wrong.

Both times, I escaped to the only space I could call mine—
tucked into silence, shaking with shame.
I didn't have the words.
Only the knowing.
Only the ache.

I needed safety.
I needed belief.
I deserved to grow up in love—and with love.

But in our family, secrets were sacred.
We buried them under school bells and Sunday shoes.

We carried them like invisible weights
tucked behind purses and pressed hair.

I kept waking up like nothing happened.
But I was already unraveling.

By my teens, the damage had seeped into every corner of me.

There were police calls.
Arguments.
Choking.
You dehumanized me—
and still, I tried to earn your love.

I was made to be a second mother
long before I had a chance to be a child.
I was responsible for caring for my sister with special needs,
making sure everything was taken care of while you were out.
But I suppose that's just what they did back in the day—
handed girls a full house and called it growing up.

I learned how to stay in open spaces.
How to always have an exit.
How to scan a room for safety.

School became my escape.
Chorus.
Plays.
Part-time jobs.
Anything to stay out of that house.

At sixteen, I got pregnant.
He gave me attention—
even if it came at a cost.

You promised to keep it between us.

But you didn't.
And just like that, my baby was gone.
And a piece of me disappeared with it.

I carried that silence, too.

You embarrassed me by your absence.
Every pageant. Every concert. Every milestone.
You didn't show up.
You didn't seem to care.

Daddy...
Why did you leave me?

Maybe I didn't deserve you.
Maybe she didn't deserve me.

By eighteen, the weight of it all collapsed on top of me.
And in the darkest moment, I considered ending everything.

I told my sister.
She told you.
And for once—you came.

The cuts healed.
Life moved forward.
But the tenderness never returned.

When I finally left that house,
you became someone else.
Colder.
Crueler.
As if freedom made me your enemy.

I think you loved him more.

Or maybe he was easier to love.

I was raised in survival.
With bruises no one could see.
With secrets no one dared to name.
With pain no one wanted to claim.

Parents—
Believe your children.
Sit with them.
See them.
Show up for them.

Because some wounds don't fade.
And some lives don't break all at once—
they unravel slowly,
quietly,
until there's almost nothing left.

I was almost lost.
But I lived.
And now—I tell the truth
so that maybe someone else can live too.

Chapter 2:

What Was Buried, Bloomed Anyway

Reflective Echo:

I was told not to tell.
Not with my mouth.
Not with my eyes.
Not even with the way I walked into a room,
holding silence like a second skin.

They said it didn't happen
if you prayed hard enough.
If you dressed right.
If you behaved.
If you forgot.

But I remembered.

Not in full sentences—
in fragments.
In the way my stomach flipped
when footsteps echoed behind me.
In the way my body flinched
when doors creaked open.

I carried bruises
no one could see.
And still, they asked
why I seemed so angry.
So closed.
So hard.

But I was not hard.

I was shattered.

Not by one moment,
but by the echo of many.
Not by a monster,
but by a village too afraid to name him.

They taught me shame
before they taught me love.
Taught me silence
before I ever learned to scream.
And yet—
what was buried,
still bloomed.

The little girl who wasn't protected
grew into a woman
who built her own sanctuary.
A woman who walked with fire in her chest
and forgiveness in her pocket.

Not for them.
But for herself.
Because some stories
will rot you from the inside
if you don't find a way
to let them rise.

Chapter 3:

Raised by My Sons

They saved me.

Not in the storybook sense of knights and castles, but in the real, gritty, tender, everyday kind of way.

They saw me before I saw myself.
They mirrored my strength when I felt like falling apart.
And in every moment that life tried to convince me I wasn't enough, they reminded me that I was everything.

Christopher came first—wide-eyed, curious, and quiet.
He taught me that love could be gentle. That presence mattered. That someone seeing you come through the door with joy could heal wounds that went unspoken.

Cortes followed—bold, vibrant, and emotionally tuned in.
He taught me that softness is not weakness. That laughter is a language. Those hugs can speak louder than words.

I was so young, still healing, still trying to become who I needed to be.

And yet—they never made me feel like I was failing.
Even in the chaos of single motherhood, of late-night tears and overdue bills, of missed sleep and silent prayers...
They gave me a purpose.

I remember holding their small hands, feeling overwhelmed at the weight of responsibility.

I didn't have all the answers, but I had love.

And love, in our house, was loud.
It danced in the living room.

It showed up in lunchbox notes and dollar store toys and made-up lullabies.

It filled up the cracks that life had left in me.
I raised them with everything I had—my stories, my strength, my softness.

But they raised me too.
They raised my self-awareness.
They raised my sense of worth.
They raised my joy.

And now, as I watch them grow into men who hold space for others, who listen deeply, who move through the world with both power and tenderness—I see the legacy we've built. Together.

If I never accomplish another thing, being their mother will always be my most divine and holy calling.

They didn't just make me a Mom …

They made me whole.

Chapter 4:

Christopher, My First Home

You were the most beautiful thing I had ever laid my eyes on.
The purest love I had ever known.
The kind of love that softened everything I thought I knew.

From the moment you were placed in my arms,
I became someone new.

A mother.
A protector.
A poet of the unspeakable.

I was only 21 years old, fresh from grief and growing pains,
still aching from the loss of my father,
still searching for my mother's affection—
and then there you were.
My son.
My salvation.
My new purpose.

I gave you everything I never had.
I didn't know how to mother from example,
so I mothered from the well of my longing—
from a place of deep yearning to be seen, safe, and celebrated.

You gave me my first real sense of family.
You were the anchor I never knew I needed.

Even when I struggled—financially, emotionally, spiritually—
you never went without love.
And if you ever doubted it,
know that you were the light that saved me from darkness.

I remember the way you smiled in your sleep.
The way you watched me with your big, brown eyes—
as if I was your whole world.
And baby, you were mine.

Christopher, I wasn't afraid to be your mother.
I was so much more afraid to fail you.

You deserved the world.

And maybe I didn't always get it right.
But I fought for us.
I stayed.
I sacrificed.

I learned how to grow up while raising you—
and in many ways you raised me too.

I found pieces of myself in your laughter.
I found faith again in your resilience.

And I found home in your hugs.

You were my first sanctuary
the place my spirit could rest.
Loving you gave me life.

Thank you for choosing me.

You were my beginning.

My why.

My first miracle.

And no matter how much *time passes* …

in my heart,
you will always be
my baby.

—Forever *Mommy*

Chapter 5:

Cortes, the Love That Completed Me

And just like that, I was about to become a mommy for the second time.

This time was different.

I was still young, still growing, and yes—I was already a baby mama by society's standards.

But my circumstances had changed.

This time, I was loved.
Loved by someone who protected me, who provided for me, who made this chapter feel safer, softer.

And you, Cortes—you were a ball of energy from the moment you started growing in my belly.

I didn't have the morning sickness I had with Christopher.

You were ready.
Ready to come into the world with a fire all your own.

At 32 weeks, I started contracting ...
Dr. Cody looked at me with that serious gaze and said,
"It's too soon, Mom. I need you to slow down."
But how could I?
I was already a mother.
I was working, building a home, doing my best to balance love and life with your father.

You were born into love.
Into care.
Into comfort.

At 36 weeks, I was placed on bed rest.
You weren't letting up.
And right on time at 40 weeks, the contractions came again—
this time for real.
Eight hours later, you arrived.

All almost nine pounds of you.

Big. Grand. Perfect.

Two days after my birthday.

The best birthday gift I've ever received.

Still are.

Even Dr. Cody smiled when he saw you and said,
"You did it again! He almost looks like a girl—he's so
precious."
And he was right.

You had the longest, curliest hair I'd ever seen.
Big, bright, round eyes that stared straight through my soul.

You were beautiful. Exceptional.

I couldn't believe I had another son so perfectly made.

And while I was caught up in your cuteness, I quickly learned
just how curious you were.

Smart. Busy. Adventurous.
You kept me on my toes.

And with every ear infection, fever, sleepless night, and teething
war—you became the second great love of my life.

You were funny, entertaining, full of personality.

All mine.
And every time I saw you and Christopher together, my heart
overflowed.

I felt blessed.

God had given me everything I needed.
And deep in my heart, I knew...

You were the love I needed to complete my home—
and to help heal the broken pieces left in my heart.

—Forever *Mommy*

Chapter 6:

My Spirit Kissed the Earth

I didn't know how much of me was missing until I walked into the trees and let the quiet wrap itself around my shoulders.

It started with a simple walk.
No plan. No playlist. Just air.

The kind that hugs your lungs gently. The kind that makes you remember your body isn't just a vessel of stress and schedules, but a home you've neglected far too long. That day, I walked like the path knew my name. Like the breeze had been waiting to meet me. Like God was whispering, "I've been right here."

For years, I moved through life as a checklist.
Mom. Wife. Leader. Caretaker.
Doing. Giving. Showing up for everyone but myself.

But something sacred happened when I stepped onto that trail.
My breath slowed.
My spirit stood still.
And in that stillness—I found myself.

Peachtree City became more than a location.
It was soil for my renewal.
I was raised in Florida, stretched in Texas, sharpened in Maryland—but I was grounded in Georgia.

I rediscovered the sacred in the ordinary. The way my hips swayed to a rhythm only I could hear. The way the sun filtered through the leaves like stained glass from heaven. The way the wind kissed my neck and made me feel… kissed.

It wasn't loud.
It wasn't grand.
But it was mine.

And in that quiet, barefooted moment of clarity,
My spirit kissed the Earth.
And the Earth kissed me back.

Not as a farewell

But as a welcome

Back to *myself*.

Chapter 7:

Sunlight and Shoulder Blades

It wasn't just lunch.

It was a soft celebration.

A moment where I caught a glimpse of the woman I was becoming—and I liked her. A lot.

We were sitting outside, the sun dancing across my shoulders, making my skin look like bronze and honey. I had on a sundress that made me feel... HER

The kind of dress that drapes just right, clinging in the places you want and flowing in the places you don't. I noticed the way the fabric kissed my curves, how the breeze flirted with my hemline, and how the sunlight made my collarbone glisten like a soft flex.

I wasn't hiding.
Not in shame. Not in size. Not in spirit.

For so long, I dressed in camouflage—oversized shirts, long cardigans, muted colors—as if softness and shine had to be earned. But that day, I wore sunlight and confidence like accessories. That day, I remembered how to show up for myself without apology.

I remember catching my reflection in the restaurant's window. My shoulders looked strong. Sculpted. Free.
I could've cried.

Because behind those shoulders was a woman who had carried so much.

Grief. Guilt. Grown woman weight and grown woman responsibility.

And yet somehow, I still glowed.

I laughed louder than I had in weeks, dipped my fork in Greek dressing, and didn't count the calories.

I didn't feel guilty for the carbs or self-conscious about the way I crossed my legs. I was just... present.

I don't know who needs to hear this, but don't wait until you shrink to start shining.

Wear the dress now.
Eat outside now.
Laugh until you snort now.

That moment wasn't about vanity.
It was about visibility.

And for the first time in a long time, I saw myself—
Not as a project.
Not as a provider.
Not as a placeholder.

But as a woman reclaiming joy.

One *Shoulder Blade at a Time.*

Chapter 8:

I Showed Up

(written from a reflection in 2017)

Last week, this time in 2017, I was with my son—standing backstage, helping him prepare for his show. He was glowing. Not just from the spotlight, but from joy.
His brother had come too, and to him, that meant everything.

He said so out loud, proudly—on social media:
"One of the best days of my life."

And in that moment, my heart knew it had done something right.

He was proud that I showed up. But what he may not fully know is that I was proud that I could. That I did.

Because I know what it feels like when no one shows up for you.

When I was eight, my father passed away. And my mother— well, that's a different kind of grief. The kind that lingers even when the person is still alive. Her absence wasn't always physical, but it was emotional. Distant. Conditional. I've made my peace with it over time... or at least I've learned to breathe around the ache.

But somewhere between that little girl being let down and the woman I've become, I made a promise. A quiet one. The kind you don't need a stage or witness for.

I promised I would always show up for my children.

Not just for the big moments. But for the in-betweens. For the dreams that scare them. The auditions. The heartbreaks. The silence. The chaos. The joy.

Because I know what it's like to scan a room and not see a familiar face. To crave applause that never comes. To want someone—anyone—to say, "I see you, baby. You're doing amazing."

My kids deserve better. And better starts with me.

I don't always get it right. I've made mistakes, and I've had to learn as I go. But what I've never done is quit. I've never stopped choosing them.

Showing up for them is my protest. My healing. My redemption.

And I don't need credit. I don't need the post or the shout-out.

But I will keep checking their timelines, smiling when they say they feel seen.

Because I was invisible once.

And now, I've made it my mission to make sure my children never are.

Originally written from a reflection in 2017.

Chapter 9:

Ode to PTC

A love letter to the quiet that saved me.

There's a kind of peace that doesn't shout. It doesn't make a scene or demand to be noticed. It just... settles in.

Peachtree City (PTC) did that for me.

I moved there during a time of upheaval, still healing from emotional wounds, searching for a rhythm I could live inside. And PTC, with its winding golf cart trails, quiet lakes, and tree-lined roads, gave me that rhythm.

It wasn't glamorous. But it was everything I didn't know I needed.

I found stillness there. I found God again in the trees. I found pieces of myself on long walks, music in my ears, tears in my eyes, joy in my belly. I waved to strangers. I smiled at the sun. I remembered what it felt like to simply be.

My days had a rhythm: morning walks, candles burning while I worked, grilled chicken and Moscato on the patio. I made peace with my loneliness. I wasn't rushing anymore. I let myself rest.

And I fell in love. Not just with a person, but with a possibility. A version of me that didn't feel lost or overlooked. A version of me that laughed more, wrote more, dreamed more.

I left Peachtree City for love, but leaving broke my heart a little.

Because I wasn't just leaving a location.

I was leaving a season that healed me.

And while I may never live there again, part of my soul still strolls those trails. Part of me is still waving at neighbors I never got to know. Still buying flowers from the Kroger off Peachtree Parkway. Still letting the sun kiss my shoulders while I sip something sweet on the patio.

PTC was more than a place.
It was a passage.

And I will forever be grateful to the quiet that carried me home to myself.

And though I left it behind,
it never truly left me.

Part II: The Breaking

Love, Loss, and Letting Go

Chapter 10:

He Didn't Deserve Me

I kept trying to be enough for someone who was never ready.

He said all the right things—until he didn't.
He smiled in ways that made me believe I could finally exhale.
And for a moment, I did.
For a moment, I let him in.

I made room for him.

I softened... again.
Stretched... again.
Believed... again.

Because maybe—just maybe—this time would be different.

But it wasn't.
He loved me in the mirror but not in the messy.
He adored my glow but not my grief.
He held my hand in the light but left me in the dark.

Still, I stayed.
Not because I didn't know my worth—
but because I thought love meant staying.

It doesn't.

Love doesn't make you shrink.
Love doesn't make you question your softness.
Love doesn't ask you to wait in agony
or confuse presence with partnership.

He didn't choose me.

And the truth is—
he didn't deserve me.

Not because I'm perfect,
but because I was real.

I brought all of me—
wounds and wonder,
fire and forgiveness,
history and hope.

And he just wasn't ready.

But I am.

So I packed up the version of me that waited.
I kissed her forehead.
Told her I was proud.

And I walked away glowing—
not because I wasn't hurt,
but because I finally stopped begging to be chosen
by someone who couldn't see my shine.

Let that be the last time I ever hand over my light
to someone who only wanted to dim it.

Chapter 11:

Do You Love Him?

The question was simple: "Do you love him?"

But it felt like a trap.

A question loaded with expectation, assumption, and judgment. Because love, at least the way people frame it, is supposed to be the ultimate answer.

The cure-all. The end goal. The reason you stay.

But what if it's not?

People give advice based on their own lived experiences.
But that doesn't make it gospel.
And what works for them may be the very thing that breaks you.

We've been taught to believe that if you love someone, you're supposed to stay.

You're supposed to work through anything.
You're supposed to sacrifice.

But why?

To reach the status of marriage?
To say you won?
To uphold a fantasy?

See... I used to believe in hopeless romance.

I was that girl—dreaming in full color, swept up in emotions, soft looks, and deep kisses.

Whimsical, wild-hearted, wanting the kind of love that fills every room.

But then I learned:
It has to be bigger than love.

Love isn't a whisper across the room.

It isn't just what you say when you're wrapped in each other at night.

It isn't just the "I love you" text or the pull between two souls.

Because love alone isn't peace.
Love alone isn't security.
Love alone doesn't clean up after itself when it leaves you shattered.

And I grew tired of people acting like love is the end-all.

Because sometimes, love comes with pain, with patterns, with cost.

And if the cost is you?
That's too expensive.

Love should not mean tolerating repeated hurt.

It should not mean carrying someone else's wounds while yours go unhealed.

It should not mean re-victimizing yourself in the name of
"working through it."

So many people are putting on for love.

Smiling for pictures, but crumbling inside.
Celebrating anniversaries, but grieving in private.
Lying to themselves, just to say they stayed.

So yes… I love him.
But I love me enough to know—
love is not enough.

Not if it comes without respect.
Not if it comes without emotional safety.
Not if it costs me my joy, my peace, my wholeness.

And no, that doesn't make me bitter.

That makes me honest.

That makes me free.

Chapter 12:

It Wasn't All Bad

I want to set the record straight.
It hasn't always been sad times.

Our initial meet-up was casual and sweet.
He was cool, mysterious, and easy to talk to.
And me? I was big light. Exciting, fun, intentional, and uninhibited.

He was drawn to my glow—and the fire he sensed smoldering deep within.

He wanted me, and honestly, it didn't take much convincing.

On our first date, he leaned over to kiss me.
It was slightly awkward—he caught his balance mid-motion—but it was sweet. Endearing.
Over time, I adored his softness.
He let me ramble, let me be my whimsical self.

Oh, the mystical, dreamy mermaid I was—ode to my Pisces sun.

We connected so easily.

He was arguably one of the most handsome men I've ever laid next to.
I would lie beside him, mesmerized by the beauty of his face—and of his spirit.

He moved through rooms slowly, deliberately.
He stood tall … confident, commanding.

And his hands… my favorite. His stance… solid. I gravitated to it.

We were beautiful together—

But those times… those early days… were good.

And before—and in between—all the times he ended the relationship ... I stayed drawn to his deep, mysterious quiet.

Our connection was passionate ... intense.
Our beginning felt like something out of another world.

Free. Uninhibited.
We created a space that was ours.
We were so grown with it.

And while some of it might sound surface,
I realized—too late—how deeply I needed those things to root into something real.
How much I longed for them to last.

But the truth came in pieces:
What he would and wouldn't sacrifice for me.
What I gave—and gave—and gave.

I was always the consistent lover.
Solid in my heart.
Unwavering in my belief that something meaningful could come of this.

He held firm to his own truths—his family, his boundaries, his pace.

But I needed to feel protected.

I needed to feel secure.
I needed less financial burden.
Mostly... I needed family.

And though we tried to navigate those gaps,
sometimes it wasn't enough—for him.
So he left. More than once.

By the time he realized he was truly locked in on me—
it was too late.
I realized it too late, too.

The inefficiencies. The missing pieces.
They still echo.

My heart still aches sometimes over what could've been.
I search for clarity.
Often, I find none.

Life brought emotional epiphanies and heart-wrenching
revelations.
Sometimes I felt dragged, re-victimized.
But love, love—always pulled me back in.

No matter how broken I felt, I stayed committed.
Committed to the idea that something had to come of all this.
These days... these nights... these years had to mean
something.

So if you ever read this, know this:
It wasn't all bad.

But eventually, as I learned to love myself more deeply,

I realized something else—

What we had was no longer enough.

Chapter 13:

In the Space Between

(Echo poem to "It Wasn't All Bad")

— for the version of me that still wonders.

There's a space between
the memory and the truth—
a flicker of light,
a hush in the room
where I remember how your hands felt
before I remember why I let go.

Where the good plays louder
than harm.

Where the warmth of your voice
briefly overshadows the silence
that followed.

I revisit the soft parts.

Not because I want them back—
but because they were mine, too.

I trace the outline of what almost was,
what never settled,
what I kept trying to shape
into something solid.

There's a space between forgetting
and forgiving.

Between ache
and acceptance.

And I've learned to live there.

Chapter 14:

Fairytales

I must've dreamed a thousand dreams of the perfect man
Kissed his lips a million times in my mind.
Imagined how he would look, how he would smell,
How the air might shift when he walked into a room.

I held tight to my fairytales,
Not because they were real,
But because I needed something to believe in.

The truth is
I was foolish.
Not because I loved,
But because I thought love alone could carry it all.

I didn't grow up seeing partnership modeled
Not the kind rooted in communication, accountability, or
emotional safety.
What I knew—consciously and subconsciously—
Was how to serve a man.
How to stay.
How to make excuses.
How to cling to toxic loyalty
Like it was a badge of honor.

And so I stayed in lingering "situationships"
Disguised as deep friendships or mature understandings
Telling myself that peace was better than clarity,
That presence was better than commitment,
That crumbs were better than nothing at all.

But I was lying to myself.

All of it was surface and polished.
And every ending still hurt like hell.

Because beneath it all,
I just wanted to feel safe.

Wanted to feel chosen.
Wanted to know that someone would protect my softness
Instead of exploiting it.

I longed for love that would wrap around me like a warm
wind—
Strong. Steady. Sacred.

But what I eventually realized is *this*:

Love doesn't look the same for everyone.
Falling in love doesn't guarantee forever.

And everything I was looking for—
The safety, the security, the certainty—
Had to begin with me.

My voice.
My decisions.
My standards.
My *healing*.

The fairy tale I was searching for?

It wasn't out there.
It was in here.

And now I'm rewriting the story—

One truth at a time.

Chapter 15:

I Cried for Miles

A letter to the version of me who kept walking, even through the ache.

Today, there's a deep, sunken sadness that lingers in every step.

I can't explain it in full, but I feel it in my bones—in the quiet moments, in the breath I hold without realizing, in the tears that almost come but don't. I just feel... sad.

And if I'm being honest, this sadness has been *building*.

I've been trying to make sense of it. Digging through the layers of guilt, regret, and memory.

And I keep circling back to this truth: I once believed marriage was the ultimate.

The final chapter of the love story I'd worked so hard to write.

But what I've come to learn is that marriage, on its own, is not the reward. The right person is.

There were signs. So many signs. But I wanted to believe in redemption and growth and love's second chances. Maybe even third or fourth ones.

When he broke up with me that second time, I was shattered. I still remember the ache in my chest. But I got up every day. I showed up for work. I walked those trails and cried mile after mile, hoping each step would lead me back to myself.

That version of me was stronger than she knew.

That should have been it.
That should have been the end.

But I kept choosing him, hoping that one day, he would fully choose me too.

And now here I am... with so many questions ... *distant*.
Connected by promises, but severed by carelessness.

I've tried to be kind. I've tried to be soft. I've extended warmth when all I've felt in return is cold disregard.

Sometimes it feels best to keep my distance ...
Not because I don't love him... but because love without safety feels like punishment. And I've punished myself enough.

Some wounds aren't just about what someone did.

They're about what they didn't protect.
What they ignored.
What they promised in therapy, then shattered with careless words.

And maybe that's why today hurts.

Because I've tried to forgive things I should've walked away from. I've tried to pretend certain transgressions didn't still echo in my spirit. But the truth is, there are things I can't overlook—not because I'm bitter, but because I'm finally being honest with myself.

I hope this feeling will pass soon.

But maybe it's not meant to pass just yet.

Maybe it's here to teach me something.

Maybe this ache is the push I need to reclaim myself.

I cried for miles.

And now… it's time I walk toward something new.

—*Christina*

Chapter 16:

The Truth Is Buried with Him

A letter to the father I lost too soon...

There's a truth I can't find.
And maybe I never will.
But if I could whisper it into the earth where you rest,
it would be this:

I want to dedicate all of my love to you.

All my devotion.
All the pieces of me that were only ever safe in your arms.

But I only had you for eight years.
And then you were gone.

And I was left with her—
the woman who birthed me.
The woman who never really saw me.
The woman who made love feel like survival.

I often felt cheated by life.

Like I was handed a story that was missing too many pages.

There's so much I don't know.
So much I've heard.
So much I wish I could ask.

But the truth is...
that truth died with you.
And the rest?
It's buried somewhere deep in the fractured memories ...

Sometimes I wonder if this is even real—this life, this ache, this history.

But what I know is:
I needed you.
I still need you.

And I wonder who I would've become
if I had been raised by the man who loved me first,
instead of the woman who didn't know how.

You are a mystery now.
But also… a comfort.

A soft, unfinished sentence in my story
that I still carry in my heart.

And maybe that's where you were always meant to live.

Chapter 17:

All I Have Are Pieces

A letter to the father whose memory is fading but never forgotten.

The images of you have faded over time.

What I can remember.
What I can recall.

It's all pieces now—soft, scattered, and sacred.

I still can't believe it's been almost 42 years.
That I've lived a lifetime without you.
That a single moment took you from me,
and the world just kept spinning.

Losing a parent that young…
it does something to you.

It carves out a space that no one else can fill.

A wound that never really heals—
just deepens quietly over time.

I remember church, walking there with you
me, you, and my sister.

I remember the stained glass windows catching the light.
I remember falling asleep in the pews
safe in your presence.

I remember your voice—just *barely*—
faint conversations on the phone,
Us, singing The Jeffersons theme song:

"Movin' on up…"

and… *Sadly*, I remember the day I came home from school,
and they told me you died.

I remember the disbelief.

Because the men standing in our apartment looked just like
you. Your brothers….

I thought—this must be a mistake.
He's here.
He's still here.

But you weren't.

And little did I know then…
how your absence
would echo through my life.

How the loss of your protection
would forever change me.

You were the first love I ever knew.

The first man I trusted.

And even as your memory fades,
my love for you remains vivid.

All I have are pieces.

But I hold them like treasure.

Part III: The Reclaiming

Voice, Power, and Return to Self

Chapter 18:

Glow Scene: The Woman Who Stayed

Dear Me, When Love Felt Like Sacrifice ...

Dear Me,

When love felt like sacrifice, you stayed.

You called it commitment.
You called it loyalty.
You called it working through it.
And maybe sometimes, it was.

But deep down, you knew...
you were giving more than you were receiving.

You quieted your voice so he wouldn't feel challenged.
You softened your truths so he wouldn't walk away.
You held back your needs so he wouldn't call you difficult.
You made the relationship easier—for him.

And harder—for you.

You made your peace negotiable.

You measured your worth by how much you could endure.
And still... you stayed.

Not because you were weak.
But because you were hopeful.

Because you believed in the goodness of people.
Because you thought if you just loved harder, softer, longer—

he'd meet you there.
But love that asks you to vanish to make someone else feel
whole is not love—it's erasure.

And you, my *beautiful self*, were never meant to disappear in the
name of devotion.

I want you to know:
You didn't fail.
You didn't stay too long because you were broken.
You stayed because you were trying.

And trying is not a flaw. It's a sign of how deeply you feel. How
fully you love.

But now you know better.

Now you understand that loving someone should never cost
you.

So if you ever start to feel that tug again—
that ache in your throat when you're about to swallow your
truth …

that slow dimming of your glow to protect someone else's
ego—

PAUSE.

And remember this version of you.

The one who left the door open for herself to come back
home.

The one who wrote this letter.
The one who finally chose peace over proof.

You stayed, yes.

But eventually… you left.

And that is where the real love story begins.

With all the softness you tried to give away,
~ *Christina*

Chapter 19:

The Love Bar

Someone said to me,

"The love bar should never be that low."

And he was right.

I thanked him for the reminder, and he replied,
"No one will be on 24/7—but making a 9 out of 10 effort is important."

That stayed with me.

Because the truth is, I've always been consistent in how I love—and how I show up.
Romanticized. Vulnerable. A bleeding heart.
Serving. Willing. Soft.

Always reaching for the magic.

But life has a way of shifting things.

You start adjusting to people who can't or won't offer those same dreams.
And then you ask yourself:
Is it a fantasy? Or is it simply a love that hasn't yet been matched?

Maybe your partner isn't the poetic type.
Maybe they don't dance in the kitchen, whisper in your ear, or plan candlelit surprises.

But becoming numb to those desires—
that's not maturity.

That's acceptance.
That's grief in disguise.
That's what happened to me.

I'm a lover of lovers.

I crave the kind of ethereal love that's mysterious, whimsical,
addictive.

The kind that makes you feel seen, wanted, irreplaceable.
The kind that says, "I'd never risk losing you."

But somewhere along the way, I stopped asking for that kind of
love.

I adjusted.
I accepted.
I submitted to the absence of it.

And in doing so, I lost parts of me.
I became numb.

Because I forgot what it feels like to have something to look
forward to—

to gush over a smile or touch,
to feel unexpected affection in the middle of the grocery store
aisle.

To hear someone say, "That's my baby," like it's the most
obvious truth in the world.

I long for a love that's never questionable.
Never circumstantial.

A love that wraps around my full existence—
not just parts of me.

Because when love is compartmentalized,
you begin to shrink.

You're allowed into someone's life—but never fully welcomed.

You're kept on the edges of joy, the outskirts of family,
witnessing a life you were never fully invited to belong to.

And once you go numb,
it's hard to find your way back to yourself.

And the ache I tried to silence?

It wasn't worth it.

It wasn't worth sacrificing the soul-deep desire
to be loved in a way that made me feel alive.

Loved in a way that celebrated my presence—
not just tolerated it.

So now? Now I remember.

I remember that I am worthy of the kind of love that doesn't
make me beg,
that doesn't ask me to settle or shrink or stay silent.

I deserve a love that invites me in.

That claims me publicly.

That whispers and shouts and chooses me… even on the quiet days.

I deserve love that doesn't lower the bar—

but *raises* the room.

Part III: The Reclaiming

Voice, Power, and Return to Self

Chapter 20:

The Glow Up Chronicles

There are moments when you realize you're becoming the woman you once dreamed of.

Not because of a man.
Not because of applause.

But because your reflection finally feels like home.

My glow up didn't happen overnight.
It didn't come from a magic product or a single fitness routine.
It came from loss.

From choosing myself when no one else did.

From crying in silence and still showing up to the world like I was whole.

But this version of me?

She's earned every curve, every stretch mark, every smile line.

Because now—I walk differently.

Not just physically, but emotionally.

I take up space.
I wear color again.
I say what I need.

I'm not shrinking in photos or playing small in rooms that weren't built to hold me anyway.

This glow isn't just about outer beauty.

It's about presence—that soft confidence that walks into a room before I say a word.

It's in the way I laugh now—loud, unbothered.
It's in the dresses I wear without the cardigan.
It's in the way I stopped explaining my "no."
It's in the peace I protect like a security deposit.

This Glow is earned.

It's Healed.

It's Holy.

Because I Built it in the Dark.

Chapter 21:

Fupa and Freedom

A letter to the body I once resented, now reclaiming.

I used to think my freedom was on the other side of skinny.

That smaller meant prettier.
That lighter meant better.
That if I could just lose the weight, the world would finally see me... *again*
and love me the way I deserved.

But then life happened...

Stress. Caregiving. Pandemic pounds.
And the kind of exhaustion that sleep couldn't fix.

My fupa became a familiar companion.

Not just the physical curve of skin and softness,
but everything it represented—
the stories I carried,
the survival I never celebrated.

For years, I wore shapewear like armor.
Tucked, squeezed, hidden.

I angled my photos.
I dressed to disguise.

I loved from the neck up.

But I'm done apologizing for the body that's carried me this far.
This FUPA has walked me through storms.

It cushioned my babies.

It survived heartbreak, breakdowns, and rebirths.

These days, I'm falling in love with my grown woman softness.

With the curve of my hips.
With the fullness of my thighs.
With the jiggle that reminds me—I'm alive.

No more shrinking.
No more dimming.
No more waiting for a goal weight to feel worthy.

Freedom looks like confidence in a two-piece.

It sounds like laughter during sex with the lights on.
It feels like joy when I catch my reflection and smile.

I am not a before picture.
I am not a "work in progress."
I am a Masterpiece in Motion.

And Baby… this Fupa?

She's paid her dues.

~ *Christina*

Chapter 22:

Sunday Morning Rituals

I made a ritual out of Sunday mornings.

Anita Baker would fill the rooms with her sweet, sultry voice—
setting the tone, creating the most beautiful vibe.

It was soft. Intentional. Sacred.

In my daydreams, Sunday mornings belong to love.
If Anita isn't playing, then maybe it's Kem,
and the song *"I Can't Stop Loving You"* …
floats through the air while my lover and I
share eggs and coffee in a conversational lush—
just… hanging out. No rush. No noise. Just us.

But lately, Sundays have felt a bit hectic.

So, this morning, I woke up and reached for my journal.
My intention was to write.
But something pulled me toward the kitchen.
And then, I chose breakfast.

My Sundays used to be quiet and slow moving …
I was always intentional about making breakfast
but over time, this stopped.

So, I leaned back into the ritual.
of Sunday morning bliss
I made blueberry muffins—
something different… a soft offering.

And I played Anita Baker.

Because even in the doing,
my spirit needed to dance.

Life is *heavy*.

My job is demanding, stressful, relentless.

And if I don't find small ways to celebrate joy—
I get lost in the week.

So now, before the TV blares with the game,
before the clanging of pots or voices in the kitchen,
before the day gets ahead of me…

I'm reclaiming my time.

With Miss Anita. With peace.

With music that touches my soul
and reminds me that I'm still here.

Still worthy of rhythm.

Still deserving of softness.

Still free.

Chapter 23:

Survival Works (*But Damn, It Hurts*)

Survival is an interesting thing.

My cousin and I talk about it all the time—how people stay married for years, decades even, fully aware they're unhappy. Miserable. Disconnected. But they stay.
And I get it.

Because leaving isn't just a decision.

It's a risk.

It's the risk of starting over as a woman who now has to:

rediscover who she is without the man she built a life with,

develop new coping skills for emotional and mental stability,

and *figure* out how to survive financially without the comfort of two incomes.

Let's be real…

At this age, most of us aren't getting child support. The kids are grown.

There's no fallback check.

Just you… and the mirror.

Unless you married wealth—and most of us didn't—starting
over means splitting what you built together:

Who's getting the house?
The apartment?
The furniture?
The comfort?

These aren't just logistics. They're grief.

But let's go deeper.

Nobody talks about what it means to survive inside a
relationship you don't want to be in anymore.

To stay quiet when your spirit is screaming.
To show up every day like it's normal—
when deep down, it's anything but.

That's the part people don't talk about.
And that's what I've lived.

I've made peace with certain things because I had to.
Because talking about it over and over was making me tired.
So I got quiet.
Told myself, "Be a big girl. Do what you need to do."
And I did. I do.

But the cost of survival is steep.

Because survival…

it asks you to keep performing in a life you no longer want.
It asks you to keep showing up in a role that no longer fits.
It asks you to keep shrinking your joy, your voice, your light—

just to make it through another day.

And the truth is:
Survival works.
But *damn*, survival hurts.

It hurts to pretend.
It hurts to stay.

It hurts to be everything to everyone while feeling like no one
sees you.

But here I am.
Still here.
Still standing.

Not because it's easy.
Not because it's fair.
But because something inside me knows:
I won't survive forever.

One day, I will live again.

Chapter 24:

Glow Scene: The Power in My Eyes

I was born with big, bright brown eyes—
passed down from my Daddy.

Eyes that gleam with curiosity in every glance,
the kind that dream dreams
from a million years ago.

My eyes have always been the center of expression—
joy and pain, wonder and warning.

They developed a vision far beyond circumstance.

I used to get teased for having big eyes—
and for rolling them.
So, I never embraced them.

But over time, something shifted.

The very thing I once felt ashamed of
became the thing I was most praised for.
And when I discovered the beauty of makeup,
I started crafting moments around these eyes—
painting, defining, commanding attention without a word.

I learned how to captivate with a soft stare,
how to silence a room without raising my voice.

I learned the mother-glare that says "Don't test me,"
and the kind of look that told my kids: "I mean business."

I learned how to seduce, with one lingering gaze…
the kind of stare that unknowingly, captivates …

Found in dreams
that haunts your soul …
in the midnight hour.

These eyes side-eye the boardroom
when my talent is tested.
They sit up tall and look through you—
through the intimidation tactics,
through the attempts to make me shrink.

Ha.

I was born with these eyes.
And they represent POWER.

The silent kind.
The kind you don't see coming,
but you feel the impact of its glow.

These eyes have carried joy—
from the first time I saw my sons' faces,
through every major milestone,
and across the peaceful hills of Peachtree City.

But they've also carried immense pain.

Memories etched so deep
it's almost too much to witness.
Some things, your eyes should never behold.

But such is life, I suppose.

Still, the magic is in allowing yourself to cry—
to shed grief from your lenses

and reclaim your vision.

To see beyond the circumstance,
beyond the trial,
beyond the challenge.

Your eyes are the light to your soul.

Don't give it away.

And never forget the power within.

Because these eyes?
They've seen it all—
the rise, the breaking, the beauty, the betrayal.
And still... they sparkle.

Still... they dare to dream.

So when you look in the mirror,
honor the story they hold.

Trace the lines of strength beneath every glance.
And remember:

You were born to be seen.

Born to see beyond.

Born to glow—with your eyes wide open.

Chapter 25:

Peace, Partnership, and Presence

I don't want chaos.

I don't want to be someone's afterthought or obligation.

I don't want to beg to be considered or shrink just to be chosen.

I want peace.

I want the kind of partnership that feels like breath, not tension.

The kind where there's laughter in the morning, warmth at night, and softness in the space between.

Not perfection.
But presence.
Because I've done the opposite.

I've been in the rooms where I was talked over, dismissed, handled.

Where love came with rules and conditions.

Where I questioned my own worth just to make the dynamic feel tolerable.

Never again.

These days, I crave something quieter—but more full.

A love that doesn't need to be explained.
A love that shows up, leans in, listens, and stays.

I want a partner who sees me.

Who hears the things I don't say.
Who asks, "What do you need today?"—and waits for the answer.

I want someone who brings ease, not anxiety.
Joy, not judgment.

Accountability, not control.

I don't want to be someone's peace.
I want to experience peace—with them.
Because peace isn't a prize we give away.
It's the rhythm we create together.

So if you ask me what I want now?

I want kindness in the mornings...

Depth in our conversations.
Laughter that lingers.
Hands that don't let go when it gets hard.

A presence that doesn't flinch when I'm soft, messy, tired, or unfiltered.

I want someone who chooses to know me—*daily*.

Not because they have to.
But because it's a *privilege*.

Love, for me, is no longer about struggle or sacrifice.

It's about being met.

Part IV: The Rising

Confidence, Clarity, and Grown-Woman Glow

Chapter 26:

The Glow in the Galaxy

A leadership letter to the women who carry galaxies within them.

They say Black women are magic...

But we are also methodical, strategic, disciplined.
We are alchemy and armor. And too often, we are exhausted.

They marvel at our strength, our spark, our softness wrapped in steel.
But rarely ask what it costs.

We carry galaxies—but no one taught us how to survive the orbit.

No one ever taught me how to lead. Not really.

I was expected to lead with excellence.
To be twice as good.
But with no coaching, no true development,
while carrying the weight of everything I was "representing."

I've led through performance improvement plans designed to break me.

Through panic attacks and *anxiety* diagnoses...
through moments where my presence in the room was treated as optional but my results were demanded.

Still, I led.

I led while nursing heartbreaks and raising children.

I led while they questioned my tone,
while still holding their projects together,
because I knew they'd hand me the fallout anyway.

I led as the only Black woman in the room—
on stages,
in boardrooms,
at national conferences,
on Zoom screens where no one looked like me.

And honey, I didn't just show up—I *shined*.

Because I knew someone was watching.
Someone needed to see what survival looks like in real time.

But I also carry the names of women who didn't get to lead this way.

Who were passed over, silenced, or punished for speaking up.

I lead for them.

And I lead for the ones who are still finding their voice.

Leadership has been both a battlefield and a balm.
It made me question everything.
But it also birthed my purpose.

So, I write this for every BLACK Woman who's been gaslit in performance reviews.

Who's been called "intimidating" just for being direct.

Who's been asked to smile more, soften up, dim down.

You are the glow in the galaxy.
The center of brilliance.
The one who knows how to recalibrate systems and still make space for joy.

Keep leading. Keep glowing.

But don't forget to rest.

Rest is resistance.
Rest is a boundary.

A declaration that I will not grind myself to dust for your comfort.

I am not a machine. I am not your miracle on demand.
I am human. I am sacred. I am enough—even in stillness.

Presence is power.

And your leadership doesn't require burnout to be real.

To the woman reading this while answering emails in her car.
To the one crying in a bathroom stall between meetings.
To the one who carries the weight of the world but forgets her own name—

Baby, you are not invisible. You are not alone.

You are the glow in the galaxy.

I see you. I am you.

~ *Christina Victoria*

Chapter 27:

Reclaiming Me

A letter to the woman who stopped shrinking to be loved.

I used to think love was something you had to earn.

That you had to mold yourself to fit into someone else's comfort.

Shrink to keep the peace.

Dim your light so theirs wouldn't feel threatened.

But I don't think that anymore.

I've learned that any love that requires the death of your voice isn't love at all.

That if you have to trade your power for presence, you've already lost yourself.

I've been there.
I've bent until I broke.
I've given beyond what was healthy, let silence replace my needs, and watched my joy drain drop by drop.

But not anymore.

Because now… I choose me.

I reclaim the parts of myself I buried to make others comfortable.

The laughter, the boldness, the sensuality, the magic.

I reclaim the right to rest without guilt.

To love without losing myself.
To say no without explanation.
To glow without apology.

They don't get to call me difficult just because I finally drew a line.

They don't get to label me selfish because I chose preservation over performance.

I reclaim my freedom.
My fire.
My feminine divine.
My voice.

I am no longer afraid of my own glow.

I reclaimed it.

And now, I wear it like a crown.
~ *Christina Victoria*

Chapter 28:

Comfort for Conversation

I didn't realize how many conversations I had settled for—until I found myself in one that felt like home.

Not because of who it was with.
But because of how I felt in it.
Seen.
Held.
Heard without having to raise my voice or explain my worth.

For so long, I confused proximity with connection.

I mistook routine texts and empty exchanges for intimacy.
I watered deserts with texts and voice notes, begging the energy to match mine.
And when it didn't, I called it complicated.
Healing.
Work in progress.

The truth is—I was just starving for real conversation.
The kind where my pauses were safe.

Where I didn't have to translate my tone or shrink my story to avoid sounding "too much."
Where my laughter didn't feel like a mask.

And then someone came along and asked, "What brings you peace?"

Not, "What do you do?" or "What are you looking for?"
But peace.

I remember how the question wrapped itself around me like a soft throw.

How it disarmed my defense and reminded me:
I deserve conversations that don't cost me parts of myself.

Not everyone who talks to you sees you.

And not everyone who sees you is willing to hold the whole of you.

I was a woman who gave too much away in hopes that someone might eventually ask the right thing, say the right thing, be the right thing.

But now?

I want more than conversations that just pass the time.
I want the kind that nourish.

The kind that makes my soul sit up straighter.
The kind that feels like someone walked into the room
and said ...
"You can set all that down now. I'm listening."

That ...
That is the kind of comfort I had always given.

And the kind I now demand in return.

Chapter 29:

No Fall-Back Plan

It's almost 4AM.

Yesterday, something shifted. A weight I didn't even realize I was still carrying started to lift—because we finally *talked* about divorce.

It wasn't loud. It wasn't explosive. It was real. Quiet. Sad. Honest. And while there's a deep love, I still carry for him, what lives beside that love is a deep reservoir of disappointments. So many, I've lost count.

And somehow, even after all the conversations, there was still so much left unsaid.

Even after all the hurt, I found myself scanning him with the kind of gaze that only history gives you. His hands. His height. The casual way he moved. Still incredibly handsome. Still the man I used to dream about. And still—not the one for me.

And that breaks my heart.

I didn't want this to be our story. I didn't want to sit with the sting of knowing we couldn't get it right. But here we are.

He said things that hurt. And maybe I did too. But what struck me most is that, at this point in life, we are simply not the same. Not in the way we view love. Not in how we process pain. And certainly not in how we show up.

He said he would be fine. That he always has somewhere to go when things fall apart.

And just like that, I saw the divide between us even more clearly.

Because I've never had that luxury. I've never had a fallback plan. My entire life has been built on the grind, the hustle, the necessity of getting it done—because no one else would do it for me.

I came from survival. He came from comfort.

And that comfort, as gentle as it may be, also dulled his sense of urgency. Of care. Of protection. Of me.

He always had a place to go. And I never had the option to leave. So, I stayed. I handled things. I carried the weight, the schedules, the emotions, the grief.

I often felt like the one carrying it all. And maybe that's because I've always had to be everything to myself.

There was no rescue. No pause. No soft place to land. And when I finally thought marriage might be it—might be my softness—I realized I was still the one holding everything together.

And maybe I was selfish. Maybe I expected too much. And somewhere in the middle of it all, I lost myself.

But I gained something too. Peace.

Not in a fireworks way—but in a quiet, still way.

My steps feel a little lighter. My back was a little less hunched.

I'm still grieving, but I can breathe again.

Maybe this letter feels scattered, like a journal entry spilling out before dawn.

But every line is honest. And maybe that's the kind of clarity I needed to give myself permission to move on.

No fallback plan. No backup life.

Just me. Choosing Peace over Performance. Truth over Titles.

And love—Real Love… over the illusion of staying just to say I did.

Chapter 30:

My Sons Were My Applause

A letter to the moment I stood in cap and gown, knowing I was never alone.

The moment I walked across that stage, I didn't hear applause from a partner or a parent.

But I did hear them—from the two boys who had always been my why.

Graduating with my master's degree should've felt like a celebration. And it did… in a way.

But it also felt hollow. Quiet. There was no family dinner planned. No partner holding my hand.

No village waiting with hugs and flowers. It was just me… and my sons. And that's when I realized: they had been my applause all along.

They were the ones who cheered the loudest when I studied late into the night.

The ones who noticed when I pushed through exhaustion to finish assignments.

The ones who saw the tears when I felt like quitting—but didn't.

I remember scanning the audience, looking for familiar faces. And there they were—two young men, tall and proud, clapping

for their mother.
My heart swelled with both pride and sadness.

Pride, because I had done something incredible.
Sadness, because I wanted someone else to be proud of me too.

There were others there that day... coworkers from a chapter
in my life I've since released.
But in that moment, none of that mattered.

They planned a small surprise lunch. Showed up with smiles
and celebration.

And what I'll never forget ... still brings tears to my eyes
was the stranger.

Someone saw me sitting there with my cap and tassel,
surrounded by joy and pride...
and quietly paid for our meal.

No announcement. No conversation. Just grace.

That moment reminded me: even when some chapters end in
betrayal, the universe has a way of reminding you that you're
still seen.

Still celebrated. Still worthy of soft surprises.

But make no mistake... my sons were my applause.
Their presence. Their love. Their pride in me.
That's what made the day unforgettable.

Because they were the ones who saw the journey up close.

They lived through the ramen dinners and the overdue bills.
They sat quietly when I needed to focus.
They hugged me when I didn't believe in myself.

And now, they stood before me as my greatest
accomplishment.

My living legacy.

Proof that I had done something right in a world that
constantly tried to convince me otherwise.

So no, there wasn't a crowd.
But there was joy.
There was meaning.
There was love.

And on that stage, with my cap tilted and my heart full,
I knew—I had never been alone.

Because my sons were always my applause.

~ *Christina Victoria*

Chapter 31:

Legacy Notes:

A reflection from Christina

I used to believe love meant sacrifice.

That loving someone meant you had to bend, shift, mold yourself into something smaller—more manageable—so they would stay. I used to think that keeping peace meant shrinking my voice, softening my truth, and ignoring my unmet needs.

But I've outgrown that definition.

Now, peace is my requirement—not a luxury. I no longer trade my comfort for someone else's convenience. I no longer silence my heart just to preserve the illusion of harmony.

In my next chapter of love—and in this chapter of myself—I want partnership.

Not performance. Not pain disguised as patience. Not silence dressed as strength.

Partnership.

The kind where presence is a given, not a gift.

Where we show up for each other not just in celebration, but in stillness.

Where there is laughter and play, but also room for grief and growth.

I want the kind of love that feels like soft jazz on a Sunday.

A warm coffee cup in my hand and a shared gaze that needs no explanation.

I want conversation that doesn't require translation.
Touch that doesn't require proving.

I want a love where I'm not asked to dim—not even slightly.
Where my glow is cherished, not competed with or consumed.

I am no longer entertaining the idea that love must hurt.
That struggle validates connection.
That withholding is romantic. **No.**

Now, I understand that peace is passion.
That gentleness is strength.
That the deepest intimacy is built in presence—in the quiet, steady choice to stay connected.

Peace, partnership, and presence.

That's what I want.
That's who I'm becoming.

And I will not settle for anything less.

Part V: The Reclaiming

Softness, Closure, and Becoming Whole

Chapter 32:

No Villains

There was no scandal.
No dramatic betrayal.

Just a series of choices—*his.*

And a silence that grew louder every time I came back, hoping
something had changed.

I went back four times.

Each time, believing maybe this time it would feel different.
That effort might finally meet me halfway.
That presence might grow into partnership.

But it didn't.

He loved in the only way he knew how.
But I needed more.

And I didn't need to guess what more looked like—I was
already giving it.

I showed up. Consistently.
I loved without needing a blueprint.
He just couldn't match that.

And the truth is:
I didn't cause the pain.
But I caused my own … staying in something that had already
shown me its truth.

For a long time, I tried to neutralize the story.
Tried to say, "We just grew apart," or "We did our best."

But that was me softening the truth to make it more palatable.

The truth is—he broke what we had.
Whether by neglect, emotional absence, or a failure to grow.
He broke it.

And I'm not perfect.
But I wasn't careless with his heart.

I didn't dishonor our story.
I didn't stop showing up.

So no, this isn't about villains.
It's about reality.

About a love that didn't rise to meet me.

About a woman who finally stopped apologizing for wanting more.

There are no villains in this version.

But there is a woman who finally chose herself.
And there is a man who couldn't.
and that's the version I will no longer rewrite to protect him.

~ Christina
*Because silence isn't the same as peace. *

Chapter 33:

Glow Scene: Beautiful Things, Empty Rooms

There's something so haunting about a beautiful thing that no longer brings joy.

Like a home with chandeliers and marble countertops, but no warmth in the silence.

Like a woman who gave everything—and now has nothing left to pour.

Like a room filled with curated pieces, soft lighting, and fragrant candles... but no peace.

That was my life.

Beautiful on the outside. Quietly crumbling on the inside.

I tried. I really did. To create joy. To make things feel full again. To give, to forgive, to stay.

But staying started to feel like shrinking.
And shrinking started to feel like dying.

I was cooking, folding clothes, writing thank you cards for other people's milestones
—and still coming home to a man who didn't see me.

There were nights I'd sit in silence after serving dinner, straightening up the house, making sure everyone else was settled—

and he'd walk past me like I wasn't even there. Like I was background noise in a life I helped build.
And the worst part is—I let it become normal.

Because I didn't want to start over.
Because I didn't want to break the family.
Because I didn't want to explain myself to people who didn't have to live with my decision.

But the truth is—I had already been living in a brokenness no one could see.

My heart was tired.
My body was tired.
My spirit was whispering, "Please don't let this be the rest of your life."

And that's the part people don't talk about.

The grief of staying.

The slow death of over-functioning for everyone else while no one is pouring into you.

You wake up one day and realize:
I'm surrounded by beautiful things… but I'm in an empty room.

Not *anymore*.

Now, I am choosing softness that includes me.

Now, I am choosing love that stays—not because it's convenient, but because it's mutual.

I'm done begging people to meet me in rooms I built for them.

This will be the last chapter I write from a place of being unseen.

I'm not just decorating anymore.

I'm *living*.

Chapter 34:

The Story That Is Sold

A Reflection on Performance, Perception, and Emotional Capitalism

It carries weight, suspicion, and truth all at once.
This story he tells. This version of our love.
It suggests performance—a curated retelling of what was,
edited for comfort and self-preservation.

A sale with no receipts.

Because that's what this is:
Emotional Capitalism.

Where my pain becomes part of someone else's pitch.
Where the truth gets traded in for a cleaner narrative—one
where he's the misunderstood heart, still searching for
something he claims he never had.

But what they don't know... and what they may never know, is
that I was the happiness.

I was the grace.

I was the stillness he prayed for and then rejected when it got
too quiet for his chaos.

And it's hard to sit with that.

Hard to know that the version of the story being told erases my
effort, my care, my staying.

That the complexity of our love has been repackaged into
something easier to digest—
a narrative where I simply didn't fit.

It's a gut-punch kind of grief—watching someone rewrite
history to preserve their image, not the truth.

Because I wasn't perfect. But I was present.

I wasn't everything. But I was enough.
I wasn't the reason he wasn't happy—he just never knew how
to hold whole.

That's the danger of selective storytelling…

It lets people feel comfort without accountability.
It lets them mourn a version of him that never existed while
leaving me to grieve a love that did.

So no, I'm not wrong for feeling a way.

Because it hurts to hear that your chapter got closed and
labeled "*not enough*," when you know you were the glue, the
grace, and the one who stayed too long trying to keep it sacred.

Chapter 35:

The Final Passage

This is not where the story ends.

This is where I PAUSE.

Where I stop gripping pain like a lifeline
and instead... loosen my hold.

Release what was.
Honor what still aches.
Make room for what glows.

You've read my becoming.
My breaking.
My reclaiming.

You've held the weight with me.

Felt the tremble in my voice.
Heard the silence between the lines.

And if you've seen yourself in these pages—
in the shadows, in the softness, in the survival—
then I want you to know this:

We are not what we lost.
We are who we chose to become after it.
We are not what they couldn't give.
We are what we now give ourselves.

This is *the* final passage—

But not the end of the journey.

Just a breath between what was
and what's *next* ...

Go forward in GRACE.

Go forward in GLOW.

You are already FREE.

If you found yourself in these pages ...

Dear Reader,

Thank you for walking this passage with me.

These letters weren't just memories...

They were my Becoming. My Breaking. My Reclaiming.

And in writing them, I found pieces of myself I thought were long gone.

If you saw your reflection in these pages—in the ache, the glow, the resilience—then this was always meant for you too.

I hope this book reminded you of your softness, your voice, your right to begin again.

And if you're still becoming, still rising—take your time.
The passage is yours now.

Keep Going.

Keep Glowing.

You're already FREE.

With love and light,
~ *Christina Victoria*

From the Glow Deck:
The First Flame

"You are not too much.
You were just too
radiant for the wrong room."

"I am no longer afraid
of my own glow.
I reclaimed it.
And now, I wear it like a crown."

"Writing changed my voice.
I don't just speak—
I resonate."

Glow Cards: The First Flame
—Self-Worth. Boundaries. Healing.

About the Author

Christina Victoria is a writer, entrepreneur, and mother of two sons who remain the greatest loves of her life.

After decades of pouring herself into motherhood, corporate leadership, and the pursuit of being "enough," she is now reclaiming her voice—and her freedom.

Known for her raw storytelling and poetic truth, Christina brings deep emotion, bold elegance, and soft power to every word she writes.

Freedom Passage is her debut memoir, written as a series of letters that explore love, loss, identity, healing, and starting over at 50.

When she's not writing, Christina is creating beauty through her coffee brand, relaunching her cosmetics line, and building her personal brand, Café Glow. She loves flowers, luxurious mornings, soulful music, and candid conversations that make women feel seen.

Through every venture, she reminds us: it's never too late to return to yourself—and bloom.

What's Next on the Passage

Coming Soon ...

The Peach Symphony — is a luminous collection of poetry, memory, and music, layered in movement, emotion, and sensory color

The Glow Vault — a collection of *soul-try* poems, sacred reflections, and lyrical truths written in the dark to help you remember your light.

Leadership Chronicles — bold reflections from the frontlines of corporate life as a Black woman navigating power, presence, and purpose.

Stay connected at **marionalexanderpress.com**

FB & IG @christinavictoriacollective.com |

Your Passage

A space for what this journey stirred in you—
what you released, what you remembered, what you reclaimed.

Your Passage

Your Passage

Your Passage

Until the next passage ...

~ Christina Victoria

www.ingramcontent.com/pod-product-compliance
Lightning Source LLC
Chambersburg PA
CBHW070629130626
46555CB00006B/2501